The Land Flipper
On
Owner Financing

By E.B. Farmer

Copyright © 2016 E.B. Farmer

All rights reserved.

Contents

INTRODUCTION 6

CHAPTER ONE: WHY OF IS GREAT FOR THE BUYER 8

CHAPTER TWO: WHY OF IS GREAT FOR THE SELLER 18

CHAPTER THREE: NEGOTIATING AND CLOSING 28

CHAPTER FOUR: TO DEED OR NOT TO DEED 39

CHAPTER FIVE: A LITTLE OFFICE WORK.. 48

CHAPTER SIX: NOTES FROM THE FIELD 56

CONCLUSION... 73

Introduction

A few years ago, I accompanied the old folks to a closing, to help them sort through the paperwork on a tract of land they were selling. Before I was able to sit down at the table, I made a comment to the closing lady about some wording I'd seen in the deed.

At which, one of the buyers – not knowing who I was – asked, "Are you a lawyer?"

"Hey now," I answered, "there's no need to insult me before we've even been introduced!"

And then I laughed. It's important to laugh when you tell lawyer jokes, on account of so many people taking them seriously.

Anyway, I'm not a lawyer and I'm not a mortgage or financing professional. But I've had a good bit of experience with owner financing (OF) over the years, as a principal on both sides of the transaction. Some readers of our first book, The Land Flipper, have asked me to slow down and start from the beginning with the concept of owner financing… so here I am.

This discussion will be mostly for houseflippers and landflippers, but also for traditional homebuyers and (newbie) real estate investors.

So, it's a primer on the subject of owner- or seller-financing. An overview. On the other hand, in Chapter Six I discuss some more advanced techniques which even the seasoned real estate investor might find interesting.

Most of my OF experiences happened years ago, and legalities change from time to time and also from place to place. So you'll need to read the dirty legal details of owner financing elsewhere – things like state usury laws or possible licensing requirements for seller-lenders or various other legal aspects of it. I'm only here to discuss how it has worked for us on the ground.

So ask one of those laughable lawyers for help before trying OF out for yourself, is my advice.

I hope this material helps you somehow.

Chapter One: Why OF is Great for the Buyer

But First: What is Owner Financing?

Owner financing (OF) is pretty simple. It's when the guy who sells you the object or service takes his money over time (monthly) rather than as lumpsum cash. Do you need some expensive mouthwork? Look around and find a dental office which will let you pay them over time for all that root-canaling and crowning. Gotta have a new refrigerator? Yeah, you might have to apply for a Sear's credit card so you can keep your milk from spoiling while you pay for the thing.

In the case of real estate (RE), the owner functions as both seller and lender, and just like a bank, she won't trust her buyer's word on the loan but will place a mortgage/lien on the property which she is selling. If the buyer doesn't pay as agreed, she'll go through a process to recover the RE.

Foreclosure is a common name for that process. Repossession.

In virtually all cases of OF, the seller will get something extra from the buyer for financing her item. It might be a higher price. It might be interest on the unpaid balance. It might be both. As usual in capitalism, those without capital (poor folks) have to pay more.

But don't be mad at the seller. Money is time and time is money. She deserves 1) her price and 2) whatever a third-party lender would make if the buyer used them for the financing, rather than using the seller for it.

With RE, the owner-financing seller will generally make the buyer sign a promissory note (an IOU secured by a mortgage or deed of trust) which will spell out all the terms of the financing:

APR... or interest rate.
Term... or how long the loan is spread out or amortized.
Payments... by the week, the month, the quarter, etc. How much, etc.

Default... including what triggers it, like failure to pay on time or failure to cover the property with insurance, etc.

Due on Sale Clause... or whether a new buyer can assume the OF loan.

And other terms.

Before we go on, let me advise again that you always use a lawyer with any and every real estate transaction, but perhaps even moreso with owner-financed deals. There may be some federal laws which are pertinent, along with individual state laws, so let the professionals guide you.

What's So Great About Buying with OF?

No Money Needed

You don't need a bunch of money to buy real estate (RE). Not if you bargain for owner financing and especially for a low downpayment. Under the right conditions, it's even possible to buy RE without any money at all up front. One time we bought a group of duplexes which were so run down that the tired old owner just wanted out. We walked away from that closing with 40 rental units and about $4,000 cash. That's because he sold to us with nothing down AND gave us all the escrowed rental deposits at closing. (40 units X $100/unit security deposits.)

Sweet.

And our rental income paid the monthly note on those places. We had to fight for it, as we worked our fingers to the bone and ruined our backs, gradually improving the units and raising the rent, but I can't remember that we ever had to reach into our own pockets on that deal.

Which was a good thing, considering the condition of our pockets at the time.

Anyway, although this is an extreme example, it is very much true that you can buy RE with little or no money down, by asking the owner to finance the sale.

No Credit Needed

So far as I know, the old man never even checked our credit. He did ask us for financial statements but, as I say, he was desperate to sell and must not have had very high standards when financing properties.

Over the years, no seller has ever again asked me for a financial statement. Not even for my social security number to run my credit.

Who knows why. Maybe because they can tell that I'm pretty professional and presumably substantial. Maybe because they don't mind if I fail and they get the property back. Or maybe it's just because they want to be done with the sale, so they can move on to other things.

I don't know. But I know that even if I had terrible credit, none of those seller-lenders would have caught me. Bad credit would not have killed any of my OF deals.

If you have credit problems or maybe you are self employed, without the ability to prove your income through traditional documentation, ask for OF. Maybe you've got a bankruptcy which won't scroll off your credit report for another two years. Ask for OF.

Not to say that a seller-lender will not run you though the credit wringer, especially on a single-family residential property. He very well might. But not usually with the vigor of an institutional lender, and he might go ahead with the loan anyway, especially with a larger downpayment or by using one of the non-deeding techniques described in Chapter 4.

No Underwriting and Bank Fees

If you've ever bought a property with traditional bank financing, you have my condolences – especially if you are a divorced woman. I once sat through a closing where a thrice-divorced woman had to tediously sign all five of her names, again and again, on dozens of documents. Most all of them were the mortgage papers, the bank papers.

And that's just the hassle part of it. There's also the money part of it. A mortgage lender will comb through every detail of your life and of the property and then make you pay for its underwriting efforts, plus various other fees. Origination fees, loan points, credit report, flood certificate, mortgagee title insurance, credit report on spouse and dog, tax certificate, appraisal fee, PMI, etc.

I've read that closing costs for traditionally-financed homes run between 2% and 5%. So buying a $200,000 home could cost you as much as $10,000 in closing fees.

But if you bought the same home with OF? Maybe as little as $500, if you just need the title search and the doc prep. A bit over $1,000 if you're wanting title insurance.

Quick Closing

Let's say you've found a property which you believe to be a most excellent deal. So good that you're worried you might lose it before closing.

A traditional bank loan could take 6 -8 weeks to close. Even longer if some minor issue comes up. A septic system in need of pumping out and recertifying. A glitch in the survey requiring negotiation with a neighbor.

What to do? Well, you could just propose owner financing to the seller. Offer a large downpayment or maybe a balloon payoff. Whatever you need to do to convince him.

You can now close within days, maybe within hours. All you need is a clean title and the proper docs prepared.

If you need to make a loan against the property later, after you own it, you could still do that and pay off your seller-lender early.

Leverage

So you've found these three great houses. They're side by side, just around the corner from your home, and belong to a doctor who lives in Timbuktu. The no-good renters have trashed the places and recently moved out in the middle of the night. You've talked to the doctor, and he really wants to sell. ASAP.

Because you are handy and have an account down at the hardware store, you are certain that you can buy these houses, fix them up, and make a really big pile of money, either on a flip or by renting them out.

The problem? Well, you're stretched out. Your banker is a little worried about you and will only make you a loan on one house… with a $15,000 downpayment.

Damn! If only I could buy all three houses! It's my shot at the big time! Right here, on this one deal! If only I could –

Oh, calm down.

And think about it. Have you forgotten about OF?

Call the doctor. Convince him to take $15,000 as downpayment on the three houses and then to receive regular monthly payments from you. (See Chapters Two and Three for ways to convince him.)

Leverage your money. Use owner financing to buy all three houses. OF is a great way to leverage yourself into bigger deals. More deals.

But wait. Is your banker right? Is it dangerous for you to do that – to leverage yourself out that way, beyond what he considers to be prudent?

Sure it can be. You betcha. Just ask anyone who got caught RE-heavy by the Great Recession.

Can you get rich as a RE operator without doing that?

Nah… not so much.

By the way, private seller-lenders almost never report your loan to the credit bureau. If you are happy to hear that, well, great. Use it as you see fit. If you're sad about it, because you want to build your credit, ask your seller-lender to please report your timely payments and help him figure out how to do that.

Chapter Two: Why OF is Great for the Seller

But why would you, as the seller, consider owner financing? Wouldn't you rather get your sales price all at once – a luscious pile of gleaming green – instead of having that money trickle in over a period of months or years?

No, not necessarily. There are excellent reasons to consider selling with OF. Here are a few:

Ease of Selling Property

You can sell a bunch more inventory if you're willing to owner finance. Just ask GM or Dell or Walmart. I think it's the biggest reason that most corporate sellers also offer financing. They don't really want to be in the money-lending business, not at first. They just want to sell more of their product.

But what if you've only got one product? One house to sell?

Well, OF can make that sale happen a lot more quickly, more cheaply, more certainly, and more easily.

Higher Price

Most buyers who need owner financing don't care nearly so much about the total sales price as they care about the downpayment and the monthly payments.

That's like an actual rule of nature or something.

You can sometimes get more for your house, or any other item, if you offer OF.

A Sure Sale: No Inspections. No Appraisal. No Survey. No Nothing.

We don't deal with VA loans or Fannie Mae, but we've heard nightmare tales about home sales bogged down or even stopped dead in their tracks because of a technicality imposed by a lender or governmental guarantor like the VA. And there is nothing more heartbreaking to a seller than spending all his proceeds, at least in his mind, and then learning that there will be no proceeds – not for a while and maybe never.

If you've got an older, out-of-shape home to sell, consider owner financing it to some hardworking young couple, but with a balloon payment due in a couple of years. That gives them time to get the home in passable shape, up to all codes, before refinancing with a VA or FHA or other conventional loan. You might even offer them an early-payoff incentive. They might save a chunk off your note balance, plus lowering their interest rate from your OF rate, down to a much lower VA or FHA rate.

So if you want your cash, incentivize them.

A Quick Sale

You can make a deal to sell your property on the weekend, with OF, and close it by Wednesday.

Try that with institutional lending.

Interest Income

Sometimes I watch a TV show called "American Greed". What amazes me is that the Ponzi promoters can sucker people into their schemes by offering a 'guaranteed' 10% return on their money.

"What!" I scream at the TV every time they say that.

"WTF?" I shout at the dog. "Did that guy just say 'ten percent'!"

I pause it, rewind and replay.

"He did! He did say ten percent! People consider ten freaking percent a great return on their money? Enough of a return to trust a huckster with it?"

(Yeah, the dog considers me hopelessly histrionic and doesn't even glance up at me anymore when I scream at the television.)

But seriously: Ten percent is very much doable if you owner finance your property. Ten percent is sometimes just the routine rate. So long as you can do it under applicable laws, a buyer won't usually balk at 10%.

And your investment is solid as a rock. A lot closer to 'guaranteed' than even the non-huckstering stock traders promise. If things break down, you can take your house back and sell it again. No Ponzi guy can run off with it in the meanwhile. Just get enough of a downpayment to cover possible foreclosure costs and damage to the property.

I've heard that some people even use this as their primary business plan.

Find a buyer who wants a $500,000 office building but can't qualify for the loan. Negotiate hard and buy the building yourself for $450,000 cash. Turn around and sell it to your OF buyer for $550,000 at 10% interest, with $50,000 down. So your $400,000 cash has turned into a $500,000 RE note at 10% interest.

Houseflippers with cash, of course, can do even better than that.

Buy a ratty old house for $100K and put $25K into fixup. Sell it for $200K with $25K down at 10%. You've turned $100K cash into a $175K note at 10%.

Landflippers with cash, of course, can do even better than that.

(Again, check on the applicable laws and work with an attorney.)

Notes Are Liquid Wealth

You can sell your RE note. We have sold good notes over the years anywhere from 75% of face value to full face value (100%).

Which means that even if your buyer has put 50% down on the property and you have absolutely no fear of his default… you should still do underwriting on him. If you decide to sell the note, the notebuyer is going to want to vet both the RE collateral and the notepayer. ***Note:*** Underwriting the buyer might even be required under some of the 'predatory lending' laws, depending on your specific situation. Check it out.

So here's the thing: If you have a $100K house and need the cash, you can maybe sell it for $110K on a note, and maybe turn around and sell that note for $100K. Especially once the note is seasoned – a year or two old, with a good performance history. So selling on a note can still net you the cash you deserve. And the sale is much easier to do, as I've described.

You can also use notes for collateral. Have you found a house to buy, but your banker wants too much on the downpayment? Let him take your existing, older RE note as the downpayment on the new house. He gets a mortgage on the new house and a mortgage (?) on the note which you already own. You'll probably keep the monthly payments on any note which you use for collateral, but you might agree to notify the banker if its balance drops substantially.

So think in terms of a 'collateral package' – which might be a mix of RE properties and RE notes – to secure a loan.

This may not be standard banking procedure, by the way. You'll probably have to find a local banker or else a commercial banker and then do some convincing. But your RE note can surely be used as collateral on new borrowing.

Better Tax Treatment

I am even less or a CPA than I am a lawyer or mortgage broker, but I'm pretty sure that your note can be treated in two different ways. You can either claim the entire principal (profit) portion of the note in the year you make it, while claiming your interest income yearly, as you receive it. Or you can break out the principal portion each year and claim it as you receive it, along with the interest portion each year, as you receive it.

Obviously I'm not an expert on this issue, but I've heard smart money guys speaking positively about good tax reasons for selling on a note rather than for lump sum cash.

Repossession

I feel guilty about it, but what can I do? A guy pays me monthly for three years and then calls me up one day saying he's getting a divorce or has to move out of the country. He asks if I'll just accept his land back instead of suing him for the unpaid balance of the note.

"But you've put all those payments into it," I say. "Can't you sell the land to someone else and recoup some of your money? I'll even let a new buyer assume the note if you like. At least get a couple thousand for your equity and let a new buyer pick up the payments."

(I'm not being a saint here. Mostly I just don't want to hassle with getting the property back and having to resell it.)

"No, sir. I've got no time. Will you take the property back without suing me?"

Yeah… I feel guilty. But what can I do? So I accept a deedback. He deeds the property back to me and I burn his note. Then I resell the property for probably more than the original sale.

We have heard of business people who make a good living out of this. They sell to poor folks in the hope that the folks will default. A good definition of 'predatory lending,' if anyone asks me. But I've heard that these guys make out real well.

Anyway, it's another possible reason to owner finance. Get a large-enough downpayment and then one day maybe get the property back to sell again.

Mailbox Money. Scale It Up.

Once you sell on a note, you've not only liquidated your property, but you've taken care of turning your cash into a solid passive investment. Two-in-one. So long as everything goes along as expected, you've got mailbox money. There's a good chance that once you've experienced a sale with owner financing, you may want to do it again. That's the dream for a lot of folks. Mailbox money.

Owner financing seems like an excellent way to get that dream started.

Chapter Three: Negotiating and Closing

How to Convince a Seller to Finance

First thing to remember is that you've got to ask. Lots of RE owners just don't understand how it works or might not even realize that such an option exists for them. Or maybe they've just got a gut reaction against hearing the term 'owner financing'. So you might need to educate them on the features and benefits for the seller as described in the preceding chapter. At the same time, during your interactions with the seller, you can be convincing him that you are a stand-up guy, worthy of the risk. Put on your best manners. You're asking the owner to place a lot of trust in you, so sell yourself.

Second thing to remember is that you may need to persist. Start early with the proposition. If they turn you down – and then have to watch as their property sits on the market for another six months, or even suffer the collapse of a traditionally-financed sale – they may soften up to your proposal. We've done that, softened up a seller over a period of weeks or months.

Negotiating with the Seller

As always when negotiating with a seller… listen.

Is he concerned about having to take the property back? Offer a larger downpayment. Describe how, as a handyman, you intend to improve the property so that his collateral will increase in value. If necessary, agree to let him keep the deed, as described in the next chapter.

Does he think that he can get more by investing his money elsewhere? Offer a higher interest rate and a balloon payment in two years. (Most especially if you're a flipper. After all, you don't intend to own the property in two years.)

Does he seem in a hurry and anxious that the property might not sell right away? Tell him that you can close next week, and remind him that his note can be sold for cash or used as collateral to borrow money.

Maybe he's got a terrible renter in the house and seems concerned about how to go about the eviction process. Tell him that you'll take care of that yourself, as soon as you buy.

Listen, and try to give him what he wants.

Contract Details

I'm not going to offer an exhaustive list of the items which you'll need to consider when creating a RE contract – things like who pays for closing, whether there'll be a survey, inspections, etc., but will focus more on the terms of the actual financing. The note.

Even so, I'll surely miss some things. Download some Deeds of Trust or Credit Sale Deeds and Promissory Notes and review them when you are preparing to make an OF deal.

But here are some high points regarding the financing part.

Downpayment

This is the big one. You'll want to put down as little as possible. The seller will want more – to assure that you won't walk away or maybe to pay off some obligation which he faces. With OF, you can usually get away with less down than with institutional lending, especially if the property needs a lot of work and can't be sold with traditional financing.

Tip: In lieu of downpayment money, offer to put some money into escrow – with the lawyer or title company – to be used only for improvements to the property. That money can't be released without the seller-lender's permission. As you bring him receipts or show him the improvements, he instructs the lawyer to release some or all of the funds, to reimburse you for that. His collateral becomes more valuable, so he becomes more comfortable about possible repossession. With land sales, we sometimes let a buyer put $5,000 into escrow, with no downpayment. When he installs a septic tank, we release $2,500 to him so he can pay for that. Etc.

Interest Rate

If you're a flipper, you just don't care much about the interest rate. Offer the seller 15% (if it doesn't violate usury laws – although that would be his concern rather than yours). What does it matter, since you're only going to bear that rate for a few months.

On the other hand, maybe you intend to pass his financing on to your buyer, by doing a wraparound mortgage or taking a second mortgage for your profit. In that case, it matters even for a flipper.

Most everyday sellers will be embarrassed to ask for more than 10%. After all, the going rate is closer to 5%. Just negotiate it as best you can, in conjunction with the downpayment, the term, etc.

Term

If you're a regular homebuyer, or a landlord, you want the longest term you can get. Better to have a 30-year note with $400 monthly payments than a 10-year note with $800 monthly payments. Most notes these days don't have any kind of prepayment penalty. (Although you should check for that.)

We've even had people who got a 15-year note from us but made monthly payments as if it was a 10-year note. You can usually pay faster if you want.

If you're a flipper, again… you just don't care very much about the term. Not unless you intend to pass that financing on to your buyer.

Balloon

A balloon payment is an agreement, a requirement, to pay off (usually by refinancing the property) at some time before the full amortized term. You can amortize the loan for 30 years but agree to pay off the entire balance in two or three years. It's something a seller-lender might want.

In our experience, a lot of seller-lenders won't enforce it. They get comfortable with the monthly notes, and with you as a notepayer, and let the balloon ride. Don't count on that, but don't stress yourself with refinancing if the seller-lender doesn't care about it anymore and agrees to waive it.

Note: Under some circumstances, balloons may be controlled or even outlawed by various laws. As usual, check with your lawyer and with typical, local tradition.

Due-on-Sale (Acceleration Clause)

So a long time ago I bought a house from a private individual and got owner-financing from him.

A couple of years later, I had to make sudden plans to leave the city for an opportunity elsewhere. I needed to sell my house on the quick.

Buyers came around, and one of them asked if he could just give me my equity and pick up the monthly payments. "If I can do that," he said, "I'm ready to buy."

I had no idea. It just hadn't occurred to me. So I called my seller-lender and asked him about it. "Nope," he said. "I want to be paid off."

Oh, boy. What to do, what to do.

So I called my lawyer, the one who had prepared the note.

"No problem," the lawyer said. "There's no due-on-sale clause in that note. You can let the new buyer assume it."

"Due-on-sale?" I asked.

"Right. If there's a due-on-sale clause in the note, then the note has to be paid off at sale. But if no due-on-sale, as in the case of this note, you can let anyone pick up the payments. It's assumable. But you're still responsible if your new buyer defaults," he added. "You signed the original note, so you're responsible."

So I had little choice but to make my seller-lender mad. I was in the legal right, even though I still feel a bit guilty about the whole mess even to today.

But from that time forward, I've tried to read my notes carefully before signing them. An institution will always have a due-on-sale clause. Virtually always. But not so with a private seller-lender. Depends on the lawyer who draws up the note. So negotiate the due-on-sale clause. (Or don't negotiate it. Just don't mention it. Often a seller-lender won't even think about it, and your lawyer can simply not mention it in the note.)

This issue of the due-on-sale clause can become very serious – especially for a flipper. I'll talk about it more a little later.

Note: It is our understanding that even institutional lenders will rarely call a note due and payable just because you're sold the property. So long as they are receiving timely payments, they may let it ride. If you are a brave or desperate person, keep that in mind.

Incentive for Early Payoff

Especially if you're a flipper, negotiate with the seller-lender for a discount in the event that you pay off his note early. Many seller-lenders will go for it, cash money being cash money and all.

As a seller-lender, tell the buyer that you'll knock off $2,000 of the note balance if he pays you off in the first year, $1,000 if in the second year, or whatever.

Partial Release Language

So let's say you bought those three houses which I mentioned earlier, from the doctor living in Timbuktu. You paid $165,000 for all three, gave him $15,000 down, and signed a mortgage note for $150,000. Good deal.

And now you've got a buyer for one of the houses. He wants to pay you $100,000.

But there's a problem. The doctor's mortgage is not a $50,000 mortgage on each of the three buildings. Rather, it's a $150,000 mortgage on the whole triplet. That mortgage covers all the buildings. It actually binds every atom of every molecule of every….

You see what I mean. So if you want to sell one of those building for $100,000, you have to pay the doctor the whole $150,000, to release that one house from his mortgage, to give your buyer a property free and clear of debt.

Well, unless you negotiated a partial release clause with the doctor and included it in the note. If you agreed, in the note, that you could release any one of the three buildings for a payment of one-third of his original note balance, then all you have to pay him now is $50,000 to release the one building.

Probably he would do it anyway. If you went to the doctor and asked him to release one of the buildings for $50,000, so you could sell it, he'd probably go along. But if you already have that partial release clause in your note, then you don't need his permission. Just deliver $50,000 to his lawyer and get your release.

Closing the Sale

One time I knew of a land developer who had a doublewide at the entrance to his subdivision. When he made an OF sale, he just walked the lotbuyer into a back office and had his cousin (also his office manager and notary) sign them up.

Don't do that. Most especially if you are the buyer. Use a lawyer. It's worth it.

Tip: Try to find one who laughs at your lawyer jokes. Those are usually the best kind.

Chapter Four: To Deed or Not to Deed

In the first place, I'm not an expert in the matter of selling RE without a deed, and in the second place, the documents seem to vary radically from place to place. My lawyer buddy calls it a 'cultural matter', which seems to mean that different areas of the country do it in different ways, with different paperwork.

Here are some names for it which I found poking around online:

Lease-Purchase

Lease-Option

Land Contract

Installment Land Contract

Contract for Deed

Rent to Own

Bond for Deed

Option

Essentially, as the seller, you can <u>retain the deed</u> to a property while conveying 1) physical possession and 2) the *RIGHT* to a future deed if certain circumstances are met – mainly being paid as agreed, but also receiving evidence that insurance and property taxes are being paid, etc.

In exchange, you get some kind of downpayment or deposit and then monthly payments.

In the old days, we did a good many lease-purchase agreements, when a buyer was especially weak, and they all seemed to work out OK. Usually we proceeded to eventual deeding of the property. In rare cases the 'buyer' walked away after some number of payments, leaving us still in possession of the property.

Why Deedlessness is Better for the Seller.

Foreclosure is expensive and slow. You might expect to spend $2,000 - $4,000 and six to twelve months, and that's if the legal guys actually take care of business and the buyer doesn't fight much, which they often don't. If they can't afford to pay you, they normally can't afford to fight you.

But with a deedless deal, you can usually just evict the tenant/buyer.

Tip: In my experience, even in a deeded arrangement, most notepayers will simply deed the property back to you when they get into trouble. They don't want to be sued any more than you want to sue them. If there's any way you can do that – convince them to deed back the property – do that.

Some sellers will use deedless deals to avoid a due-on-sale clause in their own underlying note. If there is no sale, then their original mortgage can't be called due and payable. So a seller might receive payments from a lease-purchaser and continue paying his own underlying mortgage note, pocketing the difference between the two payments. Keep in mind that an unscrupulous seller might not tell a deedless buyer about his underlying mortgage. Just one more fine reason to always engage an attorney if you are closing an OF deal or any other RE deal. The attorney should find the underlying mortgage when she does the title work, since mortgages are recorded in the public record.

If you're really, really concerned about mineral rights, you might lease-purchase a property in order to retain your mineral rights through the lease period. You could just sell with OF and reserve minerals, but with a lease-purchase arrangement, you could agree to reserve the minerals AT THE TIME OF DEEDING. In states where mineral ownership proscribes after a number of years, this could give you additional years of mineral ownership.

Why Deedlessness is Better for the Buyer.

Deedlessness means that a weak buyer can still acquire a house or other property. Since the seller is facing less risk and expense, a deedless deal is usually easier to get than conventional financing or even through OF.

Also the buyer might get into a property for much less of a downpayment.

Maybe the buyer has a bankruptcy which will scroll off his credit in two years. He might do a lease-purchase deal until his credit is strong enough for refinancing through traditional means.

A lease-purchase can be cheaper, closing-wise, than a Credit Sale with Note.

Note: I would advise that you consider the character of your 'seller' pretty closely when entering a deedless deal. People tend to remain who they are throughout their lives and in various aspects of their lives. A seller of personal integrity and good reputation is perhaps your best protection in any deal and especially in a deedless one. If something goes wrong, he will likely work out a fair solution, no matter whose side the law is on.

It's possible that when you go to get conventional financing, to convert your deedless deal to a deeded one, it might be treated as a refinance rather than as an acquisition loan, meaning that you could get cash out at closing. Research the type of deal you are about to sign and ask the experts about it and also about the following issues.

Issues with Deedless Deals

Underlying Mortgage

As mentioned, you want to be sure that the seller has no underlying mortgage. Even if you are simply leasing, rather than lease-purchasing, you can still be bitten by this one. We know of renters who have lost their leases because the owner got foreclosed. For a renter, there's not much to do about that and not so much to lose. But for a lease-purchaser, it could mean the loss of your entire deal.

If the seller does have a mortgage, and discloses that to you, be sure you understand what happens if he defaults on that underlying loan.

If you are lease-purchasing a place where the owner has an underlying mortgage, make arrangements with him to somehow update you on the status of that mortgage. Ask him for quarterly reports from his bank, for example. Spell that out in the docs you sign.

One more thing: Ask yourself what happens if your leasing owner is sued for other obligations, outside of the home's underlying mortgage, or if he goes into bankruptcy. Can the home be taken by a creditor, even though you have a legitimate lease-purchase on it? Depends. Ask the lawyer and think about this before signing.

Recordation

As the deedless buyer, you want to make sure that your documents are recorded in the courthouse. Otherwise, a bad-faith owner could sell the place out from under you. At least be aware, by discussing it with the closing attorney, as to whether your papers will be recorded of public record.

Property Taxes

Determine whether, as an undeeded owner, you can still file for homestead exemption on the home. Some counties will probably allow you to do that and some won't.

Agree with the seller about which one of you is responsible to getting the property taxes paid. If the other guy is supposed to do it, check on him. At the end of each year, contact the tax authority to make sure the taxes for that year have been paid.

Insurance

Without a deed, you may be unable to buy homeowner's insurance but will have to settle for renter's insurance, to protect your contents. But you still have to be sure that the property is covered for casualty loss. If it burns down, do you lose everything you've paid into it? Who would receive the insurance payout if it burned?

As with property taxes, keep up with the status of this insurance, even if the other guy is responsible for paying it.

Interest

Can you, as an undeeded owner, deduct your interest payments, as a normal homeowner can do? Find out about that before closing.

Conditions for Deeding

Everything is negotiable. You could sign a document requiring you to pay every last payment before getting a deed. Or you could sign a doc which requires the owner to give you a deed after two or three years of proper payments. We used to do that, deeding to the lease-purchaser sometimes after only a year or two of good behavior.

Legal Ownership & the Bureaucracy

As a deedless seller, still in legal ownership of the property, you may be asked to help out with some paperwork. If the buyer needs a building permit, for example, can he get it as an undeeded owner, or will you have to step in and pull the permit yourself? Maybe the Health Department wants the actual owner to sign a sewage permit for installing a septic tank. That kind of stuff.

Heritable Contract?

I think that most every document will contain language about selling or leasing to you and your heirs, but add this item to your list. If you die, does your family inherit your rights as a lease-purchaser? Can you pass this deal on to your Uncle Fred, or is there language about no subletting?

Chapter Five: A Little Office Work

So here's what I think I know about keeping up with notes once you've got them.

Tracking the Amortization

Interest accrues daily, so I understand it, and is paid in arrears. Rent is paid in advance, but interest has to accrue before it is paid. You lend me $10,000 at 10% for one year, and a year from now I pay you the principal plus a year's accrued interest ($11,000). But if I pay you off one month from now, I only have to pay you the principal plus one month's accrued interest ($10,083.33).

If your buyer pays you exactly as agreed, you can just print out an amortization schedule from online and check off each payment as received. But if there are glitches, you probably want to keep exact dates and amounts and calculate a running balance.

Let's say the note bears 10% interest. So the calculation looks something like this:

Balance X 10%/365 = daily interest.

Daily interest X number of days since last payment = Interest portion of payment.

Payment amount - Interest portion = Principal amount of the payment.

Balance - principal amount of the payment = New balance.

So you've got a $10,000 note, at 10% interest, with payments of $132.15 each month.

But 30 days after the closing, you get a check from the notepayer for $200.00.

$10,000 X 10% = $1,000 (**yearly interest**)

$1,000/365 = $2.739 (**per diem interest**)

$2.739 X 30 = $82.19 (**accrued 30-day interest portion of payment**)

$200.00 - $82.19 = $117.81 (**principal portion of payment**)

$10,000 - $117.81 = $9,882.19 (**new balance**)

Something like that. But don't trust me. Look it up and figure it out yourself or else turn it over to the bookkeeper. The smart number guys among you can probably take 45 seconds out of your day and write a spreadsheet formula to track it.

Late fees, I guess, would fall outside of the running amortization. We've rarely taken late fees, so I'm unsure.

Check Taxes and Insurance

As mentioned earlier, keep up with property taxes and property insurance, no matter if you are the seller-lender or the buyer-borrower. Check property taxes with the taxing authority at the end of every year. If you are the lender, and the borrower carries the insurance, have yourself added to his policy as the 'loss payee' or something like that. As the mortgage holder, you should be notified by the company if the insurance lapses for any reason.

Put this stuff on your yearly calendar.

IRS Info Forms

It used to be (and probably still is) that you've got to send an IRS info form to anyone who pays you $600 or more in yearly interest. A Form 1098. One copy to the IRS and one copy to the payer, by the end of January, I think.

As usual, don't trust me. Check it out for yourself.

Releases

If you're sold multiple properties under the same mortgage, like the doctor from Timbuktu who sold his three houses, you may be asked to release one of the properties for some amount of cash. Let a lawyer handle this. I think she might need the original note to mark it up somehow, and she'll prepare a Partial Release document for you to sign, releasing the one house from the mortgage. She'll also handle the recordation of the docs.

At such a release, your borrower might ask you to reduce his monthly payments, since the note balance has dropped so significantly. In other words, he'll ask if the term can remain the same as it was.

Unless the note contains some pre-agreed wording about it, that's up to you. If you don't allow it, your note will amortize much more quickly.

Payoff and Note Cancellation

Payoffs are like presidential elections. It ain't over until someone concedes.

We've never had a problem with a seller-lender, regarding the amount of payoff, but if you make enough notes, you may encounter a borrower who just can't get the concept. They understand and acknowledge that their note bears a 10% interest rate, but they'll insist that they've already paid you more than $10,000, so why are you claiming that they still have a balance on the note? No amount of explaining may work. Tell them to give the note and the payment record to a CPA, and you'll accept whatever the CPA says about the balance. It's rare, but it can happen.

And you can't just burn the note, of course. You have to mark it "PAID" and sign and date it and return it to the borrower so he can cancel his mortgage at the courthouse. I think that's how it usually works.

What to Do When They Don't Pay

We tend to be pretty lenient. People have financial troubles, and our note is chugging along with daily interest. We've let people go as long as six months in extreme cases.

But if they are habitual and you reach the point where you're fed up with fighting them, tell them that you're going to turn it over to the lawyers and that they (the defaulting borrower) will be responsible for your legal fees – as required in most every note.

But you know, it's just regular life out there. Rarely does anyone want to fight this kind of thing in court. In fact, I don't know that we've ever had to push it that far. I can't remember actually going through a foreclosure action for non payment.

In most every case, you can arrange a deedback.

Deedbacks

If you've sold your property on a deedless deal as described in Chapter Four, you can usually just kick the folks out with an eviction proceeding. But if it's a Credit Sale, with a Mortgage and Note, you've got to go through the long and expensive process of repossession or foreclosure. If it's a Deed of Trust, you probably don't have to go to court, but the process can be just as long and expensive. Maybe moreso.

Try to avoid that, if possible. Yes, you could come out on top, with a judgement against the borrower which you might even be able to collect. But when you look back on it all, you might find yourself whining, "Oh, if only I could have avoided all that mess!"

So negotiate a deedback with your buyer-borrower. Usually they'll just agree to deed it back in exchange for not being sued, but sometimes you might want to sweeten the pot. Up to you. All I know is that they'll run, rather than walk, to the deedback table if there is $1,000 waiting for them there. Meanwhile, I am slap-me-on-the-back happy to only spend $1,000 and a few days to get my property back.

Anyway, have the lawyer handle it. You'll need to find the original note and mark it PAID and give it to the lawyer, who will call the borrower-buyer into her office for the actual deedback signing.

Chapter Six: Notes from the Field

There's so much creativity with owner financing – mostly because your noteholder is an actual human. You're unlikely to hear these dreaded words from a private seller-lender: *"Sorry, but according to the manual, your proposal would violate company policy."*

It's just easier to negotiate and close (or to renegotiate) an agreement with a single, reasonable noteholder than with the loan department of a large institution. Sometimes you can't even figure out who's in charge at those places, much less can you make a timely deal to restructure your financing somehow.

Anyway, with a little bobbing and weaving on our part, OF has helped us win some fights way out of our weight class. So I thought I would offer three examples from the field – deals we experienced in real life which might help illustrate some of the issues I've been discussing and to highlight the power of creativity with OF deals.

I'm working from a foggy memory here and painting impressionistically, so give me leeway on the exact details.

Boxwood Circle Duplexes

We were young-buck houseflippers when I figured out the wholesale/retail angle, as it relates to RE.

OK. I'm lying. I didn't really figure it out. I took the easier route and stole the idea from one of my competitors. I watched as he bought about a half dozen duplexes, as a group, all on the same street, and then sold them back out again one by one. He told me that FHA would finance up to a four-plex for an owner-occupant.

So I went to my family and presented the theory. "Here's what we do. We buy a dozen duplexes, like you find sometimes in little circular streets or cul-de-sacs, from a single owner. Then we fix them up and we sell them again one by one, individually. And we want dumps, under-rented dumps. That's because rental units sell for a factor of their monthly rent, somewhere around 100 times their rent. So if we find some dumps renting for $100/month, we can buy them for $10,000 each, fix them up, raise the rent to $300/month, and then sell them back out for $30,000 each. And because we'll control the whole street, we can bring the area up all together. We won't need to worry about slumlords next door to us."

"But where would we get the money for that?" they asked.

"I don't know," I said. "We'll deal with that if we find a property."

So we looked around in a couple of nearby cities, and damned if we didn't right away find just the thing I had described. About 15 buildings with about 40 rental units. A mix of duplexes, triplexes, four-plexes. And they were in horrible condition.

We called the owner, the tired old man that I mentioned earlier. It turned out that he owned a small financial institution in addition to the Boxwood Circle Duplexes.

So we went to a garage sale, bought some suits and ties, dressed ourselves, and went to visit him at his office.

I think he probably figured we were trying to bite off more than we could chew. Those buildings were terrible. One lady who called us later looking for a rental unit – upon hearing that it was in Boxwood Circle – exclaimed, "Oh, no! I could never live on that street! I have CHILDREN!"

Anyway, maybe the old man didn't understand our hunger and willingness to work and figured that we'd struggle with the places for awhile and then give up and deed them back to him in improved condition. I don't know why he agreed to sell for nothing down. Stuff often happens in life and in business which couldn't have been predicted by a rational mind.

The Creative Part

After we had worked on the places for about a year, we had indeed tripled the rent and had a great rental income, much more than we needed to pay the monthly note. But even though we had stepped over the threshold into CashFlow Heaven, we found ourselves one day needing an immediate $100,000, cash. I can't remember why we needed it, but we did. And that was a very large number for us. A huge number. Where could we possibly get $100,000?

All of which is to explain why we wound up threatening the old man.

We did that by informing him of our intention to refinance his loan and pay him off.

Yep. The old Payoff Threat.

And it wasn't just a threat, but an empty threat. No bank either in its right or wrong mind would have refinanced those building for us. Not at that time, and certainly not in time to give us the $100K we needed.

But before we called the old man to wave our payoff stick, we had concocted a sweet carrot to go along with it. We put ourselves into his head and created an offer which seemed irresistible to someone in his position.

If we went forward with a refi and paid Mr. Boxwood off, on a 7% note, he would have to reinvest that money somehow, and we knew he couldn't get that rate, not on a secure investment. So we told him that if he would add another $100,000 to our note, we'd agree to raise the whole rate to 9%, not just on the new $100,000 but also on the old existing note balance.

The numbers are jumbled and half-forgotten, but I remember calculating that his new $100,000 would return him something like 17% interest. As opposed to being paid off and having to reinvest his money – with the same level of safety – at something more like 4%.

He was pinned. Helpless. He gave us $100,000 cash and added that amount to our note balance.

So instead of a $300,000 note at 7%, the old man now owned a $400,000 note at 9%. And we had no intention of owning those properties long-term. We were still flippers at heart, not landlords. We knew that we wouldn't be living under that 9% money for very long.

So win-win. Owner financing can make lots of people happy.

What I'd Do Differently Today

First, I'd probably have sold those units individually, as condos, rather than as whole buildings. The smaller you can make your widgets, the more you can get for your box of widgets.

Second, I would have been sure that the note did not contain a due-on-sale clause. We had to sell those buildings on new financing. But if we could have wrapped them around the old man's mortgage, offering owner financing to our buyers, we could have done much better on the resales.

Third, I would have worked out a partial-release deal in the original note. As it happened, Mr. Boxwood was easy to deal with and did indeed release each of the buildings from his mortgage as we sold them, in exchange for a partial repayment. But he could have played hard and forced up to pay off the entire note balance in order to release any single building from his mortgage.

The Storekeeper's Farm

When the storekeeper's heirs put his old farm on the market, we had already flipped a couple of smaller tracts. Tens and twenties. The farm was about 200 acres, and we were ready to move up.

It wasn't really a farm. Just cow pastures and woods, but it had plenty of road frontage, good topography, pretty near to town.

Anyway, we still didn't have that kind of money. We couldn't just buy it outright. So we crafted an offer to buy 50 acres of it, but with an option to buy the other 150 acres within a year. We agreed with the heirs that if we were able to buy the other 150 acres, they would owner finance it for us. We even prepared the documents to be signed in the event that we did exercise the option, appending them to the option agreement. Better to eliminate as much wiggle room as possible upfront.

Then we got to work, and it soon became apparent that we had stumbled onto something. There was a bunch of pent-up demand for three-acre tracts in the area. Within a year, we'd sold enough of the original 50 acres to justify buying the rest, and we closed on the 150 acres.

The Creative Part

Nowadays mobile home companies offer something called a 'land-home package'. They handle everything. When a customer is ready to buy a manufactured home and has found a small tract that he likes, the mobile home company will develop the tract for him. They'll install a septic tank and water well, build the driveway and housepad, put up a power pole… and then finance the whole package with one conventional mortgage. Home, land, and improvements. It means that the landowner cashes out. He gets his money for the lot when the deal closes.

But back then, no such thing as a land-home package existed, or else I just didn't know about it.

Back then, you had to finance the land for the lotbuyer. Even if he had $5,000 or $10,000 in hand, you couldn't get that as your downpayment. He had to use that to develop his lot.

So I was in a position where I had to 100 percent finance any tract that I sold.

I did have a partial release agreement with the heirs. If I paid them $10,000, I could get three acres released from their mortgage and sell it to a lotbuyer. In return, I would get a $25,000 note from the lotbuyer.

But I couldn't do that, not too many times. I just didn't have the cash.

So I called my lawyer in a panic.

"That's OK," he said. "Just go to the heirs and offer to substitute your lotbuyer's $25,000 first-lien note for their release of that three-acre lot."

"Huh?" I asked. "You can do that?"

"Sure. The heirs should be just as happy holding a $25,000 first-lien note as holding three acres of the land. Happier. It actually improves their collateral position."

So that's what we did. I delivered the lotbuyer's $25,000 note to the heirs' lawyer. He kept it in his safe and gave me a release for the three acres. Then I did that a bunch more times. I received and kept the monthly payments from my notepayers (my lotbuyers), with an agreement that if their notes got below a certain balance, I would have to rearrange things with the heirs – to make sure their collateral didn't decrease too much. I had to report the balances of those notes to their lawyer every quarter or so.

Meanwhile, I was paying the heirs a quarterly payment on their note.

Saved by the lawyer and by the creativity of owner financing.

What I'd Do Differently Today:

Well, I'd try to think further into the future. If I had done that, I could have pre-arranged the agreement – that the heirs would take RE notes in exchange for their partial releases of individual tracts.

I might even have done wraparound mortgages with my new lotbuyers. I'm not sure.

The Pineywoods 20

The twenty acres came on the market at around $120,000. Long frontage, beautiful land, nice topography. I researched it on my maps; no apparent problems. I went out and scouted it; looked good.

Our problem was that we didn't have cash that we were willing to transform into RE notes. If we had $120K to spare, and were willing to finance our lot sales, that would have worked just fine. But we didn't have it, and so I focused on trying to get the owners to finance, and in such a way that we could pass that financing on to our lotbuyers.

I called the listing agent. As we spoke, I probed him about the possibility of owner financing.

"Oh, no. The owners really don't want to do that. I'm sorry."

"Well, that price is a bit too high for me anyway," I said. "But could you let me know if there's a price drop?"

Two months later, I got an automated email from him, announcing a price drop. I called to discuss, asking again about the possibility of owner financing.

"Are you sure they won't do that?" I asked.

"Pretty sure. I mentioned it to the sellers, but they'd really rather have cash."

Two months later and another price drop. I called again. By now, the agent was taking me seriously. If a buyer keeps calling you about a property, you tend to remember him.

"Owner financing?" I asked.

"Well, maybe," he answered. "Let me check on that again."

The next day, he called back. "Would you be willing to meet with the sellers, to discuss things? They'd like to meet in their lawyer's office."

"Yes. I'll be there."

At the meeting, I tried to look and sound as professional as possible. As upright as possible. If someone's going to lend you money, make them believe in you. We generally talked and had a good meeting.

On my way back home, I got a call from their lawyer. "Can you explain to me exactly what your offer would be?" she asked.

"Well, I'll pay $70,000 cash, or I'll pay $80,000 if they'll finance it with $20,000 down. But here's the thing. Their note can't contain a due-on-sale clause. That's because I intend to sell to my lotbuyers with owner financing, but I'm going to wrap the first mortgage. I can't be forced to pay your clients off when I sell some of the land."

I could hear the lawyer thinking. It was apparent that she was having to rearrange some mental cobwebs.

"So you plan to sell a 5-acre tract for, let's say, $35,000, and take a $35,000 note. But with an underlying mortgage to my sellers for $60,000? You're not going to release that 5-acres from the $60,000 mortgage?"

"Yes ma'am. That's how it would work. My lotbuyer would buy his property 'subject to' your clients' mortgage. I think I can convince my buyers that it's safe enough to do that."

"I'm sure you can," she answered. She well-knew that weak buyers would be happy to take a chance like that – especially if they felt good about me personally – if it meant they could acquire a property.

"Well, but is that dangerous to my sellers?" she asked.

"Oh, no. It's a bit dangerous to my lotbuyers, of course, in case I default on the underlying note – which I'm not going to do – but not dangerous at all for your sellers. They'll still have a mortgage on the whole place, the whole 20 acres."

"Let me talk to them again," she said.

"Also," I added. "I'll need some partial-release language in the note. If I sell an acre for cash, your sellers will get a lump-sum payment and release that acre from their mortgage."

We got lucky. The first lotbuyer paid cash. So by the time we made a deal to sell the second tract, with owner financing, the original note was down to maybe $40K - $45K. So I sold to the second guy with a $40,000 OF note, telling him that I had an underlying mortgage for $45K or so and would continue paying it. He made me jump through all the hoops, asked all the right questions. But in the end, I showed him why there was no serious danger to him. In the absolute worst case, for example, he could free up his land by paying $45,000 to my lienholders.

Eventually we sold all the land, able to offer great financing to each of our buyers, and within short order, we'd paid off the original sellers. So all of our buyers were as safe as anyone who buys a home and gets a 1st mortgage on it.

The Creative Part

I really think we did all of that up front on this one.

What I'd Do Differently Today:

Not much. By the time we did this deal, I had suffered through so many educational experiences.

I hope this brief discussion of owner financing might help you to leapfrog over a few of those.

Conclusion

Over the years we've heard people whine that they can't sell their property, and we've heard folks complaining that they really want to buy a particular house or tract of land but just can't qualify for a bank loan. I've heard it so often that my reply has become somewhat formulized: *Given a willing seller and a willing buyer, there is almost always a way to make the thing happen.*

For most people, real estate is the most valuable item they'll ever buy or sell, so every RE transaction deserves some hard thought and creativity. Knowledge is power. Ideas are power. A new and creative proposal or a bit of contractual maneuvering can be the difference between finding your way to success vs. sitting on your hands and watching the world go by.

So the next time you are confronted with a problem sale or purchase, try reviewing this book and others on the issue of owner financing. Create a proposal for your buyer or seller and persistently pitch it. You might be surprised. We have often been.

If you'd like to offer suggestions for our next edition of this book, or if you have questions or anecdotes about owner financing or real estate in general, feel free to email us directly at **info@landflippers.com** We really love hearing from people with something to say about our book, questions about their own flip deals, or even those just wanting to say hi.

We also have a more general book about land flipping, titled **The Land Flipper: Turning Dirt into Dollars**. It lays out the business with much larger strokes. You can just search for it on Amazon.

We've also recently released a 15-hour course that lays out the land-flipping process in great detail. It is the knowledge and work of about forty years of flipping, explained in plain English. It is already a cheap course, but I usually give big coupons to people who Email me and ask nicely, so let me know if you are interested. You can learn more about the course at **www.landflippers.com.**

We also blog and offer consulting services. You can check out more at our personal page:

www.thelandflipper.com. Sign up for our mailing list there if you want to hear from us more often.

And lastly. If you liked the book (or have something critical but constructive to say about it) please leave us a review on Amazon! Reviews are the lifeblood of indie-publishers like us, and we really appreciate it when people take the time.

Thanks for reading. Good luck with your real estate endeavors.